# Earth's Ecosystems

by Barbara Fierman

PEARSON
Scott
Foresman

DK

# Places For Living Things

Living things get what they need from where they live. A living thing's **environment** is everything that is around it. Plants and animals are living parts of an environment. Some nonliving parts are sunshine, water, soil, and weather.

Sunshine warms the air, water, and soil. It allows plants and animals to live in those places. Water and soil are important parts of the environment. Water falls as rain and snow. It goes into the soil. Some soils hold a lot of water. Other soils hold very little. Plants need different types of soil.

Climate is the weather a place has during the year. In some places, the climate is cold and dry. In other places, the climate is hot and wet. Many places have climates with changing seasons.

A moose's environment is a coniferous forest.

# Parts of an Ecosystem

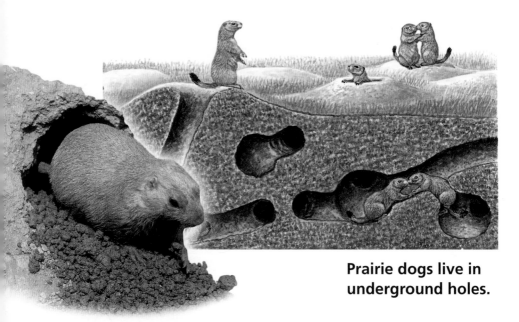

**Prairie dogs live in underground holes.**

Plants and animals live where they have water, food, and shelter. An **ecosystem** contains all the plants, animals, and nonliving things in an environment. The different parts of an ecosystem work together.

Prairie dogs dig holes in the soil. This gives the soil more air. The air helps the grass grow. This makes more grass for animals to eat.

The living parts of an ecosystem also need each other. Burrowing owls and other animals often use the holes dug by prairie dogs.

# Special Homes

Every plant and animal lives in a specific place. This place is called its habitat. Living things get what they need in their habitat. Plants get light, air, water, and space to grow. Animals get food, water, and a space to live and grow.

If one part of a habitat is taken away, the habitat will change. If prairie dogs leave their habitat, the animals that use the prairie dog holes might have to move or find other places to live.

**The cactus lives in a desert habitat.**

# Groups within Ecosystems

**African elephants**

The elephants live by a lake. They live together. The elephants are able to get water and rest at the lake. They take care of each other. The elephants make up a **population.**

Birds come to live at the lake. They make nests nearby and find fish in the lake. Other animals find food at the lake too. The elephants, birds, and other animals each belong to their own populations. Together they make up a **community** of animals. The animals in the community need each other and the lake in order to live.

# Ecosystems Change

Sometimes ecosystems change. First, one part of the ecosystem changes. Then the other parts change too.

Long ago, many wolves lived in Yellowstone National Park. The wolves ate elk and other animals. People wanted to get rid of the wolves. They killed many of them.

When the wolves were gone, there were not enough animals to eat the elk. Yellowstone's elk population grew out of control. There were too many elk and not enough food. Many of the elk died. Finally, people decided to bring wolves back to the park.

**Gray wolf**

# Grassland

A **grassland** is a large, flat area of land that is covered with grass. There are grasslands all over the world. The grasslands of North America and Asia usually have cold, snowy winters and hot summers. African grasslands are much warmer.

In some grasslands the soil is too dry for trees to grow. Trees need more water than the grassland gets.

During the spring and summer, it rains in the grassland. The rain soaks into the ground. The grasses have long roots that go deep into the ground. These roots can get water in the drier seasons.

Some grasslands get more rain than other grasslands. Tall grasses can grow in these grasslands. Short grasses grow where there is less rainfall. Wildflowers grow in grasslands too.

Many animals live in a grassland ecosystem. Rabbits, deer, and prairie dogs eat the grasses. Foxes, snakes, and other animals eat the smaller animals. Birds such as owls and sparrows also live in grasslands.

**American bison, or buffalo, live in the grasslands of North America.**

# Desert

A **desert** is a place that gets very little rain. Most deserts get less than ten inches of rain each year. During the day some deserts are very hot. At night it is much cooler.

The plants and animals in the desert need each other. All of the desert's living things have found ways to stay alive without needing much water.

One kind of desert plant is the cactus. Cactuses keep water in their stems. Their roots spread out to get water from the soil.

Desert animals hide when it is hot. Some sleep in the shade of plants. Others, such as some frogs and toads, dig tunnels under the ground. Desert animals such as snakes and coyotes often go out at night when it is cool to hunt for birds and other small animals.

When days are hot, the rattlesnake hunts at night.

# Tundra

The Arctic **tundra** is a very cold and dry ecosystem. It is located near the North Pole.

Winters on the tundra are long and cold. Some snow falls, and it is very windy. The days are short, and the nights are very long. For many weeks the Sun does not shine at all. The ground below the surface is frozen all the time.

Summers on the tundra are short and cool. The days are long and sunny. In some places, the Sun shines twenty-four hours a day. The snow melts, but the soil under the surface stays frozen.

Many plants, such as trees, can't grow in the tundra. In fact, the word *tundra* means "treeless land."

Other plants, such as grasses and wildflowers, can grow there. These plants are small and have short roots. Many tundra plants have tiny hairs on their stems or leaves. The hairs help protect the plants from the wind.

In the summer, ponds form on the tundra. Ducks, geese, and other birds make nests near the ponds. There are many insects to eat during the tundra summer. Most of the birds in the tundra fly to warmer places in the winter.

Lemmings are small animals that live in the tundra. They dig in the snow to find grass, moss, and twigs to eat. They have thick fur that helps keep them warm.

**Most of the tundra's flowers and plants are small. This helps protect them from the strong winds.**

# Coniferous Forest

Earth has many different kinds of forests. Each forest has its own plants and animals.

Coniferous forests grow in places with warm summers and cold, snowy winters. Most coniferous trees have leaves that look like needles. Spruce and pine trees are conifers.

Coniferous trees grow close together. This helps protect them from the cold and wind. It is hard for plants to grow under conifers. They don't get enough sunlight. Moss, however, grows beneath these trees.

Many animals, such as bears, live in coniferous forests. Bears have thick fur to help them stay warm. Birds eat seeds from the trees in summer. Some of the birds fly to warmer places in winter.

# Deciduous Forest

Deciduous forests grow where it rains in the summer and snows in the winter. In the fall, the leaves on deciduous trees change color. They change from green to yellow, orange, or red. Then the trees drop their leaves. In the spring, they grow new leaves that stay green all summer. Both oak and maple trees are deciduous.

It is easier for plants to grow in deciduous forests. Flowers, ferns, and moss grow on the deciduous forest floor.

Many animals live in a deciduous forest. Insects, birds, and small animals make their homes in the trees. Many small animals eat the trees' leaves, nuts, and seeds. Owls and foxes live in deciduous forests. They find squirrels and other small animals to eat.

# Tropical Forest

Tropical forests grow in places that are mostly warm and wet all year long. The trees that grow there are very tall. Some tropical forest trees are as tall as a ten-story building! The leaves on top of the trees keep much of the sunlight out. Many plants can't grow under the trees because they don't get enough sunlight.

Some plants can grow on the branches and trunks of the trees. These plants are called air plants. They get water and food from the air. Vines also grow on the trees.

Many animals live in the tropical forest. Most live in the trees. Frogs and spiders live under the leaves. Ants and beetles live under the bark. Snakes wind around the trunks. Monkeys swing from tree to tree, and colorful birds sit on the branches.

Many, many insects live in tropical forests. How many? So many that scientists haven't even named them all!

**Many tropical forest insects are hard to see. They look like sticks or leaves.**

Orchids are air plants.
Their roots dangle
in the air to get food
and water.

# Freshwater Ecosystems

Some ecosystems have fresh water. Other ecosystems have salt water. In some places fresh water and salt water come together.

Lakes, ponds, rivers, and streams are all freshwater ecosystems. Lakes and ponds have land all around them. In rivers and streams, the water moves from one place to another. The water in some lakes and rivers comes from under the ground. The water in others comes from rain or melting snow.

A **wetland** is land that is covered by water most of the time. Trees, grasses, and plants grow in a wetland. Many animals live there too. Some wetland birds have long legs that help them walk in the water. They have beaks for catching fish to eat. Wetland frogs and toads can live in the water and on the land.

The largest freshwater wetland is in Brazil. Many large rivers run through Brazil. When it rains, these rivers can overflow, flooding the surrounding land. The flooded land becomes a wetland habitat for many plants and animals.

Many birds stay in the wetlands of Brazil for a short time while they are traveling to other places. Many fish live there too. The wetlands of Brazil are also home to capybaras. They have webbed feet, like a duck. Their webbed feet help them swim.

**Capybaras' eyes and ears are on top of their heads. This helps them to see and hear when swimming.**

# Saltwater Ecosystems

Earth's oceans contain salt water. They cover most of the planet. Near the land, the ocean is not very deep. Clams, crabs, and some kinds of fish live there.

Far from land, the ocean water is deep. Large fish, sharks, and whales can live in deep water. The deepest parts of the oceans are dark and cold. Plants do not grow there because there is little sunlight.

Rivers flow into oceans. The fresh water from rivers mixes with salt water from the ocean. When this happens, salt marshes are formed.

A salt marsh is a type of wetland. Most of the salt marsh is covered with water. Many grasses grow in the salt marsh. These grasses can live in water and soil that is salty.

Some of the animals in the salt marsh are so small that you can't see them. Many sea animals start their life in salt marshes before moving out to the ocean.

**Flamingos eat the tiny animals and plants found in salt marshes.**

# The World Around You

We have now talked about many ecosystems. Yet there are still thousands more, found all over Earth. Ecosystems are everywhere. But they are difficult to define and measure because they are always changing. Climate changes. Hurricanes, and volcanic eruptions change ecosystems. Human activities and the interactions between plants and animals also change ecosystems.

**Coniferous forest**

**Grassland**

**Desert**

Ecosystems' constant changes can be difficult and confusing to track. Many people try to get rid of that confusion by thinking of Earth as one big ecosystem! However you like to think about it, one thing is for certain: ecosystems need to be protected, so every living plant and animal can have a home.

**Tundra**

**Tropical forest**

**Wetland**

# Glossary

**community**   a group of different types of animals living together in one place and needing each other to live

**desert**   a place that gets very little rain

**ecosystem**   all of the different plants, animals, and nonliving things in one place that use each other

**environment**   everything surrounding a living thing

**grassland**   a large, flat area of land that is covered with grass

**population**   all the living things of one kind in one place

**tundra**   a cold and dry area where some part of the ground or soil is frozen for the entire year

**wetland**   a land that traps water or stays covered in water for most of the year